SUBURBAN HAIKU

POETIC DISPATCHES
FROM BEHIND
THE PICKET FENCE

SUBURBAN HAIKU

POETIC DISPATCHES
FROM BEHIND THE PICKET FENCE

by Peyton Price

RUNNING PRESS
PHILADELPHIA · LONDON

Published by Running Press,
A Member of the Perseus Books Group
Illustrations by Mike Lowery

Books published by Running Press are available at special discounts for bulk pur-
chases in the United States by corporations, institutions, and other organizations.
For more information, please contact the Special Markets Department at the
Perseus Books Group, 2300 Chestnut Street, Suite 200, Philadelphia, PA 19103,
or call (800) 810-4145, ext. 5000, or e-mail special.markets@perseusbooks.com.

ISBN 978-0-7624-5380-1
Library of Congress Control Number: 2013956837

E-book ISBN 978-0-7624-5381-8

9   8   7   6   5   4   3   2   1
Digit on the right indicates the number of this printing

Designed by Amanda Richmond
Edited by Jennifer Kasius
Typography: Jump Start and Gotham

Running Press Book Publishers
2300 Chestnut Street
Philadelphia, PA 19103-4371

Visit us on the web!
www.runningpress.com

DEDICATED
to the
JONESES

WELCOME TO SUBURBIA!

What brings you? Culture? Cuisine? Community?

No, of course not. You're here for the children. Children need big yards, safe playgrounds, and excellent schools. Don't you watch *House Hunters*? Of course you do.

So you know that moms need walk-in closets (preferably with chandeliers), ample free minivan parking, and updated kitchens with custom backsplashes. Dads need maintenance-free new construction with just an hour's worth of lawn to mow, so they have plenty of time to entertain friends in their outdoor kitchen or man cave.

Congratulations! In the suburbs, you can have it all. Kind of.

This book is your guide to the three stages of suburban existence:

1. Boredom
2. Disbelief
3. Assimilation

I've seen some poor souls trapped in Stage 1 and Stage 2, dear reader, and trust me, it's not pretty. Don't let this happen to you. Pick up this book and get oriented to your suburban surroundings as quickly as possible. I've laid it all out for you as simply as I can: in haiku. These tiny descriptions of the dilemmas and dramas of suburban life will prepare you for what's in store (mostly big box stores to tell you the truth).

Or, if you have already setttled here (and you do know what I mean by settled), these little poems will set you straight with a flash of recognition and the startling realization that you are not navigating the mean streets of suburbia alone (figuratively speaking, that is—as you can see, there are plenty of cars).

If I can help just one parent through karate class, it will all be worth it.

CONTENTS

Part I
HOME FRIED...12

Part II
THESE ARE THE PEOPLE IN MY NEIGHBORHOOD ...40

Baby, Boom

After School Special

Drive Ways

Green Lite

Yard Sticklers

By the Bylaws

HOME FRIED

So it's finally dawned on you that your
take-home pay is depressingly close to what you shell
back out for child care. Or, desperate to leave the rat race,
you've promised your spouse you'll take on the cooking,
cleaning, and other even less appealing marital duties.
Or you plan to work from home after the baby's born,
taking calls during your cherub's regularly scheduled
morning and afternoon naps.

Or maybe you're an established SAHM, reading this
book because the cable's out and you're trapped at home
waiting for the guy to show up already. (How is it possible
to miss a four-hour window, I ask you?!)

However you ended up at home sweet home, everyone shall smile upon you and tell you how "fortunate" and "blessed" you are to be able to stay at home during this "special time" with your children. You are supposed to "enjoy it" and "treasure every moment" because "time goes by so fast."

Are they crazy? Anyone who says "the time just absolutely flies by" has obviously never spent an entire day waiting for small persons to fall asleep. And wake up. Over and over. Maybe the years slip by (or maybe I just can't remember them on account of the sleep deprivation) but the days, the hours, the minutes, tick . . . tick . . . tick . . .

Like loads of laundry through the dryer, these are the days of our lives.

BORED
GAMES

• • •

The dog stares at me
while I pretend I'm asleep.
We both have to pee.

• • •

• • •

Two cups of coffee
wake me up enough to ask
"Did I have coffee?"

• • •

I don't like your tone
reporter on NPR
saying "sub-urban."

• • •

Almost lunch hour.
Time to start calling his cell.
"When do you get out?"

We're out of hummus?
Now what the @#$% do I do
with baby carrots?

• • •

When I feel cheeky
and nobody else is home
I smack my own butt.

Still searching Etsy
for the perfect size tote bag
to store my tote bags.

When nothing's cooking
I cause a stir on Pinterest:
"You can buy extracts."

• • •

Did the power blink?
No. It was just me blinking.
Did the power blink?

LAZY HAZY DAZE

● ● ●

I greet each morning
with motivational thoughts:
Today is trash day.

● ● ●

It's perfect weather
for sending the kids outside
and watching TV.

To punish myself

for wasting time on the couch

I pick crappy shows.

● ● ●

This cat's so lazy!

She lies around all day long

right on top of me.

Deleting selfies.
These angles aren't flattering
my new pedicure.

• • •

Another one? (sigh)
National Geographic
is a guilty read.

• • •

Hey, look, it's Wednesday.

This week has been productive.

Good job, Mucinex.

• • •

● ● ●

I do feel better
after those thirty crunches.
Chips are delicious.

● ● ●

CHORE
WARS

• • •

Just tidying up
before the cleaning lady
who is also me.

• • •

Cleaning the ice box
makes me feel so domestic.
I just said "ice box."

• • •

I went to law school
but the highlight of my day?
Dumping the Dyson.

• • •

It takes having kids
to truly appreciate
Magic Eraser.

• • •

• • •

The kids fought so much
I made them clean the bathrooms.
(I love clean bathrooms.)

• • •

My husband asks me
"Why is stuff strewn all over?"
My answer: "Strew you."

• • •

Sometimes he'll vacuum
but he doesn't do dog beds
furniture or floors.

Inside this hamper
there's something making me gag
each time I walk by.

● ● ●

When I'm in a snit
I throw away recycling.
Haha! Take that, Earth!

MOTHER NATURE

• • •

Daffodils and I
exchange sympathetic nods.
We peaked too early.

• • •

• • •

Bird feeder battle:

New neighbors versus the squirrels.

Spoiler: The squirrels win.

• • •

I always wonder:
If a tree falls in the burb
did it hit my house?

I keep a close eye
on the hummingbird feeder.
Yep. It's still putrid.

• • •

The full moon last night
was so very beautiful
according to tweets.

ROAD TO NOWHERE

• • •

Today is the day
I gun it on this speed hump!
Shoot. No it isn't.

• • •

This car full of boys
smells like McDonald's french fries.
No one had french fries.

• • •

Waiting to turn left
I always use my blinker.
%^&* deer never yield.

It's best just to wave
at every gray minivan
and all small beige cars.

• • •

When I ignore her
she gets a little snippy:
GPS lady.

Roadways have black ice.
Should this make me more nervous
than regular ice?

• • •

Rats. A speed camera
and the limit's 25.
Hope my picture's good.

THESE ARE the PEOPLE in My NEIGHBORHOOD

As it turns out, you can't stay in the house forever.

At first, you will venture out for some retail therapy at Target—or on a really bad day, Nordstrom.

After a while, you might attend a homeowner's meeting to seek approval for that wider driveway, because although you'd think two cars would fit in a two-car garage, apparently the developer didn't anticipate bicycles or lawn mowers or the kayak you haven't used since you moved here. (Good luck with that driveway variance, by the way.)

Your precious little one will start preschool, then beg to sign up for enriching activities with brand new BFFs. How can you say no? We don't want our children to be social outcasts do we? No. We do not. Plus, who knows? With encouragement and the right teacher, your child could grow up to be a soccer star, violin virtuoso, or prima ballerina!

Next thing you know, it's time to register for kindergarten. The PTA will smell the fresh meat—I mean . . . optimize recruiting opportunities—and make you an offer you can't refuse. (I really can't say anything more about this or I could wake up with a twenty-cup percolator in my bed.)

As you face the prospect of getting to know your neighbors, you're probably anxious about whether the pop culture suburban stereotypes are true: Ticky-tacky conformity, cutthroat but entirely pointless competition, and bless-your-heart condescension. Overindulged babies who grow up to become entitled teens. Disaffected Stepford Wives and hyperinvolved Helicopter Moms.

Let me set your worried mind to rest. These ridiculous depictions are true.

BABY, BOOM

• • •

Expecting their first
they purchase the best car seat
and an Escalade.

• • •

Waiting for a sign
she asks her baby ten times
"Do you want more milk?"

• • •

VIP babies
must be en route somewhere posh
in those pedicabs!

For the bored toddler
plain Goldfish crackers are out
and iPhones are in.

● ● ●

The moms do hard time
behind a one-way mirror:
Tiny Tot gym class.

Tutus at the park
because pretend play's vital.
Plus, such cute pictures!

• • •

Party promoters
tempt with gluten-free cupcakes
and a good floor show.

• • •

Those preschool biters
can't shake their reputations.
It's best if they move.

AFTER SCHOOL SPECIAL

● ● ●

The stiletto'd mom
sized up the muddy playground
and said "Not today."

● ● ●

• • •

Bolting from the bus

he runs to mom, arms open.

"Where is the iPad?"

• • •

Kindergarteners
need help finishing homework.
"Mom! What's my login?"

• • •

He brought home classwork
that had been peer edited.
She wrote "I hate this."

Give your friend answers
and he'll call again today.
Teach him to Google . . .

● ● ●

Five houses over
it's time for trumpet practice.
That kid really blows.

DRIVE WAYS

• • •

Sounds like the neighbors
leaving now for karate
need a belt replaced.

• • •

You're so important!
Why else would you drive so fast
when you leave for work?

• • •

Traffic circle rules:
Look left for oncoming cars
then curse and floor it.

The first one to blink
wins the parking lot standoff
where someone backs out.

• • •

Mercedes ladies
may look good, but they don't look.
Be careful at Saks.

• • •

Hey, nice parking job.
Did you pay for both spaces?
It looks like you did.

• • •

GREEN LITE

• • •

Where's the Land Rover?
We decided to go green.
(Sure. With gas money.)

• • •

● ● ●

Paper or plastic?

I choose plastic, for dog poop

and get the stink eye.

● ● ●

Organic café:
The crowd is self-satisfied
(but not satisfied).

• • •

At farmers' markets
the flower stalls draw big crowds
of Instagrammers.

• • •

Mr. Bikes-to-Work:
Did your face freeze in the cold
or are you that smug?

• • •

YARD
STICKLERS

● ● ●

They replaced their lawn
with another sodding lawn!
The grass is greener.

● ● ●

• • •

The ground troops debate

use of chemical weapons

in the war on weeds.

• • •

A neighbor asked me
what I've got in my garden.
"The deer sure love it!"

• • •

Coyote urine
effectively repels pests
who stick their nose in.

With storms rolling in
he decides it's time to mow.
And look! Have a jog!

• • •

He staked his boundary
with six orange reflectors.
Now dogs mark each one.

BY THE BYLAWS

• • •

PTA meeting:
"Why can't this school be nut-free?"
Good question, lady.

• • •

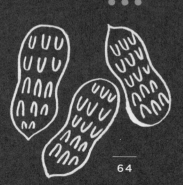

Desperate for quorum
on a vote to hike the dues
they proffer "Light Snacks."

• • •

At every meeting,
there's always one royal pain
who's read the bylaws.

Homeowners meeting:
Two hours on door colors?
Now I'm seeing red.

● ● ●

A point of order:
The chair does not recognize
how useless this is.

• • •

The neighbor who says
"Are you making a motion?"
is our cutoff man.

• • •

TEST PATTERNS

• • •

"She's repeating math
to build up her confidence
after last year's B."

• • •

• • •

**First graders receive
their reading group assignments
and sort themselves out.**

• • •

If two-thirds of kids
are in the advanced math class
aren't they average?

• • •

The advertisements
in the high school newspaper:
Test prep and nose jobs.

• • •

"For the AP test
we did a two-week prep course
and an iPad app."

• • •

At grade school book fairs
the number one bestseller:
scented erasers.

• • •

The PSATs:
Overachievers panic
at "Write in cursive."

• • •

Testing is over!

Now teachers can show their stuff.

Mostly videos.

• • •

TEEN VOGUE

• • •

Teens swarm the Starbucks
for FaceTime with BFFs
who couldn't make it.

• • •

She used her friend's phone
for an emergency call:
"Mom! I need a phone!"

• • •

Half-naked teen girls:
Extra coats of mascara
do not count as clothes.

● ● ●

A bumper sticker:

BE CAREFUL—TEENAGE DRIVER

on a brand-new Jag.

● ● ●

Her name is Kaylee spelled C-a-g-h-l-i. By whom, exactly?

KNOW
THE SCORE

• • •

Team uniform day:
One of the dads keeps asking
"Can I get a hat?"

• • •

The coach moved practice
a half-hour drive away
to a "better" gym.

The coach Replies All:
"We can help drive anytime.
Just call my wife's cell."

● ● ●

The team mom e-mails
the third and final spreadsheet:
Schedule of Drinks/Snacks.

A first-grade coach asks
"What are we going to do?"
One kid says "DESTROY!"

• • •

A swing and a miss:
the humiliating whoooof
from the parents' bench.

• • •

● ● ●

Travel team tryouts:
Kids wear their All-Star jerseys
to show they're playas.

● ● ●

• • •

Minivan window:
"Swim Fast 8 and Under Girls!!!"
(Forget you, 9–10s.)

• • •

● ● ●

Pumped up for the meet
with loud music and face paint
the moms take their marks.

● ● ●

• • •

**The swim team parents
grill for hours between heats.
I'll have a hot dog.**

• • •

• • •

At the team banquet
some of the dads are grumbling
about trophy size.

• • •

FOR ALL APPEARANCES

• • •

Nordstrom dressing room:
"This can't be a size zero!
It seems way too big!"

• • •

She tells the waiter
each of her food allergies.
She should just say "food."

• • •

"This one is so me."
She finally found her match:
trendy nail polish.

From the pedi chair
she tells her nail technician
"You should get highlights."

• • •

Ladies at the spa
moaning "I soooo deserve this"
most likely do not.

A pretty penny:
Sixty bucks on hair products
for a natural look.

• • •

At Hair Cuttery
it's fun to watch moms' faces
when they're asked, "You, too?"

PART III

RESISTANCE IS FUTILE

People who live in glass houses shouldn't throw stones.

And people who live in cookie-cutter suburban houses shouldn't write haiku about people in the neighboring houses because when your kids are about twelve years old, they will become familiar with the meaning and proper use of the word "hypocrite."

Yes, yes. I know. I was so smug. So critical.

But I have a very good explanation! Think about it this way: How could I convey the unwritten and complex etiquette of suburban life if I hadn't learned the rules firsthand? How could I help you navigate the congested roads of suburbia if I hadn't piloted my SUV back and forth across the very same hazardous landscape? How could I prepare you to defend against the tactics of PTA ladies and travel team coaches if I hadn't once been defenseless? How could I empathize with your desires for acceptance, success, and hardwood floors if I didn't share every one of them?

Really, dear reader, it was a major undercover operation *for your benefit*. Now that I think of it, you should be thanking me, not shaking your head like that.

O, how the mighty have fallen.

ERRAND GIRL

● ● ●

A smoothie is great
when I don't have time for lunch.
And then I eat lunch!

● ● ●

• • •

Rummaging around . . .

Where's my phone? Did I leave it?

Oops. I'm on the phone.

• • •

• • •

Three big SUVs

are parked side by side by side.

"Mom! I can't get out!"

• • •

• • •

Sunday Target run:
I wanted to make good time.
&$%! this church traffic.

• • •

I curse the Escher

who designed this weird garage.

Where is Level 4?

They have nice cheese there
but we can't go to Whole Foods.
We're out of t.p.

• • •

Buckle your seat belts.
Our next stop's the other side
of this parking lot.

• • •

• • •

Power through it, Mom.
Don't think about it. Just do.
Eating McDonald's.

• • •

LAWN DARTS

• • •

A muddy wet spring
is God's way of punishing
those who park on lawns.

• • •

Wrinkling up my nose
at the yards that have new mulch
and the yards that don't.

• • •

Wish my magnolia
could get a look at this one
to see how it's done.

That lawn is gorgeous.
Look at those dandelions
at the peak of bloom!

• • •

A light leaf cover
is good for the garden beds
and bugging neighbors.

• • •

Just an inch of snow
and the perfect lawn next door
looks the same as ours.

• • •

SCHOOL
HOUSE

• • •

Let's see that class list!
Friend...she's weird...friend...don't know her...
Checking out the moms.

• • •

• • •

Back to School Breakfast

Back to School Night, School Picnic

I need new clothes too!

• • •

I have a question
about my child's schedule.
Where is Honors Lunch?

● ● ●

For first-grade homework
searching for family photos
where my hair looks good.

Note from the teacher:
Your son's losing his temper.
WHAT IS THIS ABOUT?

• • •

**Did you pay our dues?
It's PTA meeting night
and I have some gripes.**

• • •

• • •

The neighbors might call
to carpool to school tonight.
Better leave early.

• • •

SHALLOW END

• • •

These pool umbrellas
don't offer much protection
from the other moms.

• • •

Thank God he's not friends
with that popular in-crowd.
(Why don't they like him?)

• • •

Which one is your son?
That one, with the Bieber hair.
Wait. No. That's not him.

• • •

Two days at the pool.

Two days of diarrhea.

That's just how it works.

• • •

• • •

**Thunderstorm warning!
Kids, be sure to play it safe
and save your games now.**

• • •

TEAM PLAYER

● ● ●

Waiting at a field
chatting away with my spouse
at a different field.

● ● ●

. . .

New water bottles:

Steel, filtered, BPA-free.

They'll all be lost soon.

. . .

• • •

Teams go by color
but it seems so wrong to say
"Go, white team! Yay, white!"

• • •

I love the playoffs.
Every time I hear "clinch it"
I do a Kegel.

• • •

It's a bit nippy
up in the stands this evening.
Too many small dogs.

• • •

The game's picking up!
The gossiping dads are here
with news of lawsuits.

• • •

• • •

Our team showed great speed
and talent for boxing out
(at the postgame snack).

• • •

LADIES AUXILIARY

• • •

Here's our donation
to the grade school rummage sale!
(Junk we bought last year.)

• • •

For tonight's potluck
please mark what is Gluten-Free
so I don't eat it.

• • •

"So-and-so told me
you'd help with the class party."
What'd I do to her?

• • •

I can only join
a PTA committee
with one member: Me.

• • •

No more free riders.
Give money for teacher's gift
or you're off the card.

• • •

Clean room established.
We follow strict protocols
for bake sale brownies.

• • •

We own this corner.
Move along now, Cookie Girl.
Take your cookie sheet.

• • •

Our campaign complete
I launch an early first strike.
It's thank-you note war!

• • •

MRS.
MANNERS

• • •

I always panic
when this neighbor approaches.
What is his dog's name?

• • •

. . .

First rule of book club:
We don't talk about the books
when we're at book club.

. . .

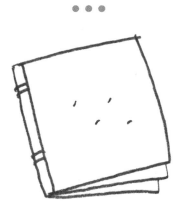

Excuse me, ladies
gossiping incessantly.
Would you please speak up?

• • •

For your own safety:
On a wet crowded pool deck
voices do carry.

Dare I say something?
I think her carpool "conflict"
is hating carpool.

• • •

"Mr. and Mrs."
means no kids are invited
especially ours.

I feel terrible.
I called my son a moron
with the door open.

• • •

It's family time.
Put away all those gadgets
and watch this TV.

• • •

**That Whole Foods trail mix
is for this Friday's playdate.
Just have a Pop-Tart.**

• • •

BETTER HOMES

• • •

We have new neighbors!
I'm so excited for them
to see my mudroom.

• • •

I always select
ultra-high-end finishes.
They're the best value.

• • •

Convincing my spouse
we needed new countertops:
harder than granite.

At Target for socks
but we do need a blender
and patio chairs.

• • •

Every October
something just comes over me.
I need tiny gourds!

• • •

Our festive mailbox
is attracting party guests
to the wrong driveway.

• • •

FINAL OFFER

●●●

The window's open?
The neighbors heard me moaning
over *House Hunters*.

●●●

A new For Sale sign.

Two doors over. Such a shame.

I heard they were nice.

• • •

What is their address?

Pull up the online listing.

YES! Interiors.

———

Click satellite view.
That must be our cul-de-sac.
Hey! They have a pool?

• • •

At open houses
neighbors sign in with fake names.
I use Real Housewives.

"Now they've stooped too low."
We exchange harsh appraisals
of our neighbor's price.

• • •

Country? Seaside? Woods?
Since *Newsweek* ranked our high school
we can never move.

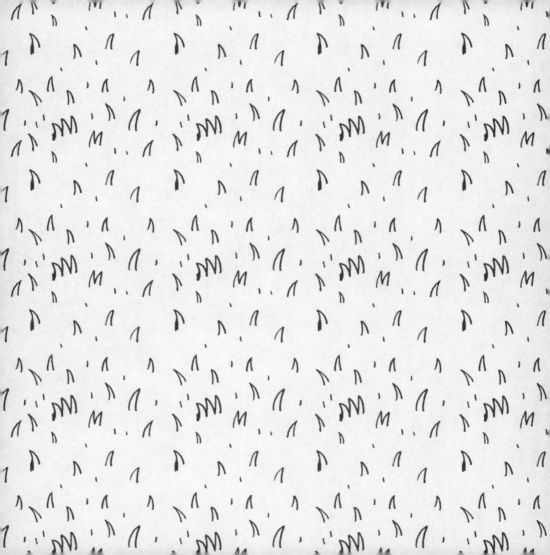

ABOUT THE AUTHOR

Peyton Price still thinks she could have been a contender. Instead, she's living the American dream in suburbia (of course) with her long-commuting husband (of course) and two above-average children (of course). She is a PTA insider, Target shopper, SUV driver, Starbucks aficionado, travel team mom, and all around suburban cliché. Her special skills include getting the worst end of the deal in every single carpool and not realizing she just replied-all to a group text. She is currently focusing on her next project, her sons' SAT scores.

Readers have asked her "Are you my neighbor?" "Are you following me?" and, uncomfortably often, "Are you inside my house?" Officially, her answer is "No comment." But you might well spot her tapping out syllables, taking a quick over-the-shoulder-peek, and whipping out her smartphone to tweet a haiku. When your curiosity reaches ex-boyfriend levels, start your stalking at suburbanhaiku.com.

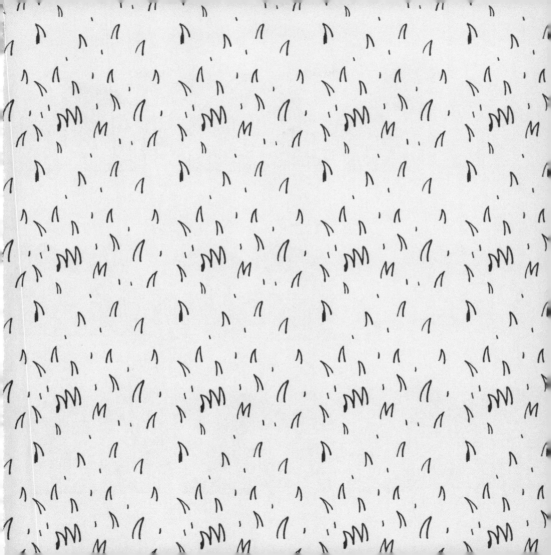